Celebrating Norouz
Persian New Year

Story and crafts by:
Yassaman Jalali

Pictures by:
Marjan Zamanian

Hi! My name is Roshan. I am 6 years old and live in San Jose, which is a large city in the northern part of California.

Every year on the first day of Spring, my family celebrates the Iranian (or Persian) New Year: Norouz. Norouz means "new Day" in Persian. Iranians have celebrated the beginning of Spring for thousands of years. I think having a New Year when the whole earth is waking up is great.

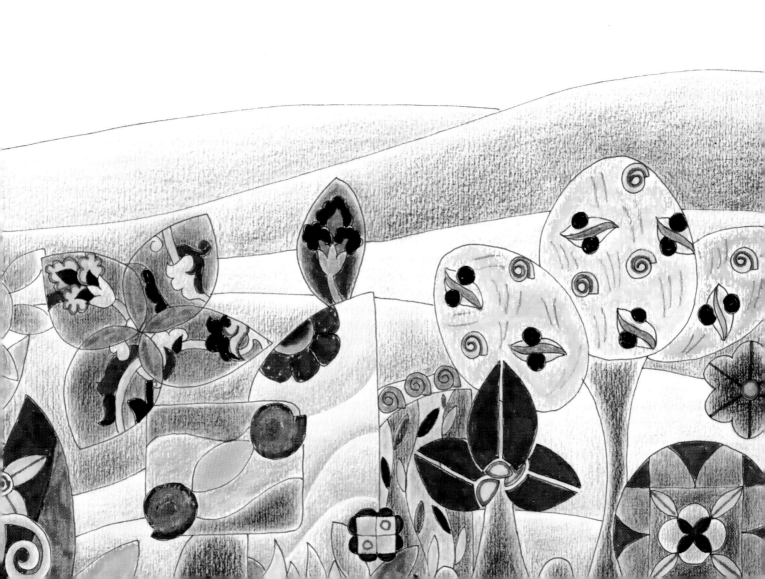

Two weeks before Norouz, we start getting ready. I help my Mom soak some wheat seeds and then spread them on plates in the sun. This will help them grow.

We also go to our local Iranian grocery store. We buy pastry, apples, candles, flowers and little goldfish in a round jar. The store is crowded with people talking and shopping for Norouz. On our way back home I get to hold and watch the little goldfish. When we get home my dad and I color eggs. I get to draw faces and rainbows on mine.

A day before Norouz, my Mom and Dad tell me it is time to help put the "Haft Seen" on the table. There are seven things on the Haft Seen that start with the letter S in Persian. My Mom tells me they each represent something special and bring luck for the coming year. We spread a colorful cloth on the table and put the Haft Seen on it.

The seven special things on the Haft Seen are: Hyacinth (a pretty flower), Vinegar, Wheat sprouts, Senjed (dried fruit), Sumac (a kind of spice), garlic and apples. We also add flowers, pastry, colored eggs, gold fish, a mirror, and pictures of our close family members who can not be with us for Norouz.

On the day of Norouz, we all put on our new clothes and my dad gets our camera ready. I notice gift wrapped boxes placed by the Haft Seen. I know many of them are my Norouz gifts from my parents and other family members. We light the candles and watch the local Iranian television program.

Exactly at the moment when winter changes into spring (it is called the Equinox), the TV announces the end of the old year and the beginning of the new one and starts to play a happy song. We all get up and hug and kiss each other. My parents have tears in their eyes. I think they miss our relatives and friends who live far from us. We take pictures around the Haft Seen to send to them.

My Mom and Dad start calling on the phone to wish their family and friends a Happy New Year. We will visit the ones who live in San Jose later today or on the weekend. I start opening my presents. This is my favorite part of Norouz!

Sal-e No Mobarak!

Happy New Year!

Craft number one:
Decorating the Haft Seen

Materials needed:
Copies of the Haft Seen picture
Crayons
Glue
Fish Crackers

Directions:
Color the Haft Seen.
Glue the fish crackers inside the fish bowl.

سال نو مبارک

Happy Norouz

Sprouts
سبزه

ried fruit
سنجد

Sumac
سماق

Vinegar
سرکه

Apple
سیب

Garlic
سیر

Eggs
تخم مرغ

Hyacinth
سنبل

Craft number Two:
Colorful eggs

Materials needed:
Glitter
glue
crayons
scissors

Direction:
Paint and color the eggs.
Glue some glitter on the eggs if you like.
cut and paste the eggs on the platter.

سال نو مبارک

Happy Norouz

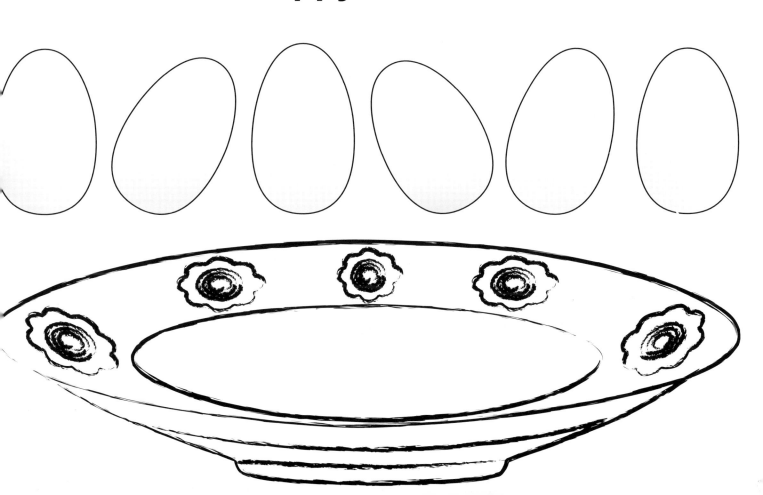

Craft number Three:
Connect the dots from number 1 to number 27 and see it grow!

Now color it green and red!

سال نو مبارک

Happy Norouz

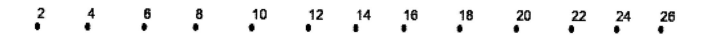

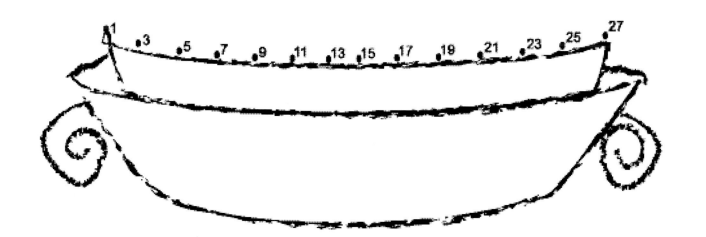